You

Must

Remember

This

You

Must

Remember

This

Poems

MICHAEL BAZZETT

MILKWEED EDITIONS

Published 2014 by Milkweed Editions
Printed in Canada
Cover design by Mary Austin Speaker
Cover photograph by Alec Soth (Magnum Photos)
Author photo by Leslie Bazzett
14 15 16 17 18   5 4 3 2 1
First Edition

Milkweed Editions, an independent nonprofit publisher, gratefully acknowledges sustaining
support from the Bush Foundation; the Jerome Foundation; the Lindquist & Vennum
Foundation; the McKnight Foundation; the National Endowment for the Arts; the Target
Foundation; and other generous contributions from foundations, corporations, and individuals.
Also, this activity is made possible by the voters of Minnesota through a Minnesota State Arts
Board Operating Support grant, thanks to a legislative appropriation from the arts and cultural
heritage fund, and a grant from the Wells Fargo Foundation Minnesota. For a full listing of
Milkweed Editions supporters, please visit www.milkweed.org.

Library of Congress Cataloging-in-Publication Data

Bazzett, Michael.
  [Poems. Selections]
  You must remember this / Michael Bazzett. -- First edition.
     pages cm
  Includes bibliographical references and index.
  ISBN 978-1-57131-474-1 (paperback) -- ISBN 978-1-57131-930-2 (ebook)
  I. Title.
  PS3602.A999A6 2014
  811ʾ.6--dc23

                    2014019175

For Leslie

II

III

You

Must

Remember

This

After Machado

Standing by the water
I remembered

the delicate and confused
dream I had last night

it was bruised
even in the remembering

so these words
can only glance

sidelong at the beehive
that replaced my heart

with all that pulsing
making honey from the loss.

I

In Vladivostok

The woman in the dream
said be careful with your cock

and I suddenly knew
in the way one knows in dreams

that my cock had somehow become
a lever that might detonate

a string of bombs riddling the city
in the way blood clots might lace

a body in its final days.
When I realized I was holding

a rooster, I did not exactly
know what to say. Perhaps

I smiled. I don't know.
There was no mirror

and I've never been able
to see myself in dreams.

Cyclops

The story is such a story we don't always stop to think
about what it was like to be there: that cavern floor
packed with pungent dung, dark as the inner bowels
of an animal when that slab dropped into place: how

utterly it sucked to hear the oaf stirring in his stupor
made uneasy by wine mixing with the bolted flesh
of good friends dispatched while we watched—
it was just a flat-out bad deal for everyone involved.

Polyphemus messed with no one: a law unto himself
there in the hinterland eating goat cheese by the ton
and Odysseus brimming full of the sauce of himself
after out-clevering all Ilium by nestling in the stallion.

He'd had plenty of time to think there in that hollow
belly smelling of fear and fresh sawdust holding his
piss in one endless clench counting droplets of sweat
rivering cold over his ribs and under his breastplate.

And now here he is again groping for his sharpened
pole in pitch dark using one appetite to feed another.
He lays the point in the drowsing embers and jostles
it enough that the cave appears in a blood-warm glow.

You probably know the rest—plunging the blackened
tip through the eyelid, the crackling hiss as the eyeball
burst, the geyser that shot from the socket—then huge
hideous blind rage: it was easy to get inside, he thought,

the real trick comes in the getting out: words that might
land differently if you are not clinging to the fetid locks

under a ram, knees pinning its rib cage, your hips held
high as it drags you slowly into the chill morning air.

Maybe then you'd feel the warmth of Polyphemus's
wounded breath, washing across three thousand years
as he crouches above you, stroking the woolly backbone,
inquiring why this particular one lags so far behind?

The Field Beyond the Wall

We walk to the edge of town: there
just beyond the wall we see clouds
of crows and ravens, also buzzards
teetering down to pick apart the flesh
that peeks from every flapping shirttail.

See that belly pale as risen dough?
The dark oaks creak with the dead
weight that hangs from their limbs—
ropes taut with bodies barely turning.

We gather on the wall, idly and in pairs,
looking out across the charred fields
and the smoking timbers of a farmhouse.

By noon, the hum of flies will lull our ears
into dreaming orchards thick with bees,
but now in the chill of morning it is mostly
the scrape and croak of birds just starting in.

Someone has knotted an enemy banner
to the tail of an ass to drag the muddy lanes.
But the ass stands rooted in a ditch,
shredding weeds with a ripping sound.

Up on the wall, a woman works the crowd,
making the rounds with a steaming sack of corn.
People buy a roasted ear for warmth,
holding it snug inside their hands for a long while
before peeling back the damp husk.

Memory

It was not yet light.
I heard my father stir.

I crept downstairs
in my pajamas to listen
as he sent my brother
to find his spirit animal:

If it is a crow it is a crow,
and you will not go hungry.

I want it to be a bear
or a wolf, my brother said.

If it is a crow it is a crow,
murmured my father.

The door whuffed shut
and cold ascended the stair.

After a long moment
I walked into the kitchen
where my father sat.

I want to seek mine, I said.

Your what? he asked.

My spirit animal, I said.

He laughed and pointed
to the broom closet.

Check in there, he said.

*Maybe the mop bucket
will be able to teach you
how to hold your water.*

Very funny, I whispered.

My father shrugged,
*What do you expect?
You're a closet Slovakian,
and your brother is simple.*

*Last week at the library
he checked out the phonebook.*

As my father spoke,
I heard the staccato
footfalls of my brother
and his curious gait.

The door burst open
with a gust of cold:

A bus! he said. *Huge
as the sperm whale!*

*The mirror of my soul
is a crosstown bus!*

My father smiled,
Good for you, Jeffrey!

His face was frank
as an open sail. Then

he looked at me and
mouthed these words:

The steam that blows the whistle
never turns the wheel.

Now that I am a man,
I can clearly recall
how snow sifted sideways
through the air, how

I never had a brother,
how my father yearned
to be elsewhere, how

I longed to board that
crosstown bus and sit
quiet in the weak light,
using a stubby pencil

to draw the curious
members of my new
family, smiling there
on those paper napkins.

Soirée

Your humor is deft and cutting
my fingers off one by one,
she said as we left the party.

I started up the car and said:
Every joke holds one blade inside
the breast pocket of its coat

to open things and liberate
the world of unremembered light.

This exchange took place without words.
A snowbank leapt into the headlights.
The car seemed to know the way home.

Until that moment I had been waiting
to put my mouth over her mouth
and breathe the ferment of the evening.

This might have led to touching
the soft parts of our bodies together.

Instead we fell asleep, tongues
heavy in our mouths like fish.

When They Meet, They Can't Help It

His obsession is a cart drawn by muscled oxen
over rain-softened roads. Salt marsh spreads evenly
on either side. Reeds stir like fine hair in the breeze.
The land seems flattened by the heat. The wheels
crush white bits of shell into densely packed mud.

Her obsession is a small animal gathering seed husks
in tunnels beneath the snow. The owl listens for the
dry scrape and scuttle. The bird blinks once as the
animal stills. The images collide here, in this moment.

The cart on the road is real. It exists in the resolute now,
drawing sand toward a work site near Dakar, where the
driver will sell it cheaply to make substandard cement.
The owl and the small animal are real as well, moving
through boreal forest in Siberia, they possess a reality
of sinew and ligature, of worn tooth and cracked beak.
Without these images, neither obsession could be seen.

The man lives to deepen grooves. The woman offers
motionless chill to mask her alertness. He is attracted
to this stillness at the coffee shop, sensing the appetite
through faint chemical signals that stir both arousal
and fear—if pressed, he could name neither impulse.

His persistence seems to her a steadiness that could
calm. Conversation over coffee leads to a coupling
neither can quite believe, a coupling in which they
open like strange flowers. In the emptiness afterward,
while the silence holds, he thinks of what they've done
and is aroused once again. It seems that he will do this
forever, in and out of years, until she is an old woman.

She looks at the ceiling and wonders, What's the sound
skittering across the roof? A cloudburst? A raccoon?
If either speaks, this will come to an end. These things
are fragile. Yet just as he opens his mouth, an airliner
thunders overhead. It cancels all sound and saves them.

Clockwatcher

The night is not a hole
to fill with your thoughts.
It is not a sock to stuff
deep in the gob of morning
and hope the sun has
soiled itself there on the couch
where it collapsed after the gin.
The sun can be so tiresome.
The night is not a black dog
snuffling around the muskrats.
The night refuses to stumble
through Byzantine circuits
like loose electricity. The night
has no limbs. It never stutters
or grabs. It settles in like
a headache: there before
you know it then a pressing
darkness stained with light
and you wish you'd taken
that handful of crumbling
white pills before it came.

Atlas

When they lead you into the room with the blind man
and let him drag his hands across the landscape of your face
so that you can smell his old skin and those yellow nails
that have begun to curl like claws, you will stand straight
and still and swallow your revulsion back into your throat

because once he has confirmed the bones of your face
fall into line with his memory of the bones of your father,
he will offer a tobacco-stained smile and a wine-tinged
exhalation and announce, yes, you could only be *his* child,
all the while fumbling for the greasy string around his neck
to withdraw from inside his shirt a key that still holds
the warmth of his chest when he drops it in your hand.
The map is in the box, he'll say. The box beneath the bed.

You expected worn parchment or carefully folded vellum
but not this sturdy clothbound book. It is not merely a map.
It is an atlas, replete with indexes, charts, and translucent
overlays that display your various organs, followed by veins
and arteries traced in red and blue, and then the delicate lattice
of nerve endings that lace your body. The fine white crescent
scar on your forehead is indicated with an asterisk to footnote
the make and model of the car door that delivered the blow,
back when you were a boisterous child. The final overlay
takes care to reproduce the actual melanin of your skin tone
and quietly highlights this fact by including a small inset box
that offers the proper ratio of ocher to umber so that the hue
can be replicated by the paint department at any hardware store.

The thought of inhabiting a room the exact color of your skin
crosses your mind. You flip to the index and begin thumbing
through the italicized headings. The word *orgasm* catches your eye.

It is followed by a list of subheadings tucked into parentheses:
(first, last, multiple, most sustained, most frightening, inadvertent,
nocturnal, diurnal, induced by: stuffed animals, Bulgarian cuisine,
silk bedding, musical role-playing fantasies, velvet; see also: *sneeze.*)
It is all here, you realize. The manual you suspected and sought.

With a start you flip to the final section, and see it bears the title:
Future Accomplishments. You are uncertain whether to continue,
knowing that the first item on the list could quite possibly be,
1.) *Currently Reading Future Accomplishments* and no matter how
quickly you begin skimming over the text your eyes will alight
upon only those words, and you will settle into a whirling pause
which comprises the rest of your life, reducing it to an infinite
bumper sticker: The Future Is Now, Is Now, Is Now, Is Now

but if you do proceed you will be delighted to discover this is
not the case. This is not some sort of cheap rip-off of Borges:
there is actually a numerical list of deeds, some quite surprising.
It gratifies you to know you will one day befriend an orangutan.
Of all the things on the list, this is the one you will carry with you
once the book has been returned and the lock has clicked shut.
Many years later, while those at your bedside await your last breath,
you remain serene. There has been no orangutan, you murmur.
No orangutan whatsoever. In this moment, you begin to recover.

The Difficulty of Holding Time

The silliness of clocks and watches,
weather vanes with no wind, spinning
to correlate a thing they don't measure
but suggest. Perhaps a large ceramic
bowl with its round mouth opened
always to sky would be more accurate.
Days pass: the sun rides its staring white
road. And *again*. Always *again*, opening
and closing like a dutiful flower. You
put entire hours in your pockets and later
find nothing but lint. You slip a minute
into your coin purse and it transforms
into foil wrapper. You chant *is* and *is*
and *is* which already *was* before touching
the world. Such relentless translation:
a well-trained man with a gun cannot
stop it, neither can a word carved
into a mountain, nor mountain itself.

The Same Bones

the face slack and whiskered in silver
the sag of the curtain beneath the eyes

the crepe-paper crinkle of skin in the hinges
the translucent browning vellum of the pate

the signs have been coming for some time

and now his ridged skull is rising
up through his softening features
like an anchor drawn hand over hand into the light

the clay of his face has grown tired
enough that nothing firm will emerge
until its bones are freed to tumble in the river

he knows me, this man

well enough that I crave his good opinion

we share some version of the same bones

having fathered the same children
with the same woman in a shared bed
though neither of us necessarily knew it

at the time: this is not a new form
of perversity but an old one

a mirror with an unusual time signature
delivered by means of a story

in which I somehow gaze upon the man
I will become

and though I can press my fingers to the glass
there is not a question I can ask that he could answer

without falling into crude pantomime
or mouthing platitudes of the moment
so we simply stare

into what we hope is the intelligence of one another's eyes
as we once did in the primate house

that time the orangutan sidled up to express
what struck us then as such a peculiar interest

tapping persistently from the inside
until at last we understood
and lifted our wristwatch up to the glass—

Some Party

Ah, tomorrow, said the important guest.
Though the day has yet to be seen,
the evidence of its existence
is well documented in the folklore of your people.

Then someone said, Tomorrow is an animal
that can be tracked but never captured.

So this cold night may not end, murmured the hostess.

I sleep deep in these long nights, someone said,
and when I wake I still want more.

The hostess nodded knowingly
and the rest of us went to the window
and watched the moon scrape itself
clean on the snow outside, while bits
of white hair sifted from the chimneys,
signifying an indifferent wind.

Thick candles stood on tables, alongside bowls
of salty nuts stirred by the fingers of strangers.

Someone said shells serve as coffins to the wind
and the white smoke we were watching
was the soul leaving the body of the house.

Some party, I said, actually beginning to wonder
if the night might not end and the whiskey
might run dry. I imagined falling

asleep deep in the upholstered couch

and waking to the darkness of the same party,
candle wax spread on the bookshelves,
embarrassed headaches, raised eyebrows

but then someone said, Look, and pointed
at the table where the important guest

was riding the hostess, her breasts quivering
like twin gelatins above the punch bowl
and I knew the night would end
before I ever saw such beauty again.

The Building

sense of momentum
as he entered the strange city
                              crowded with buildings

prompted him to lean forward to ask the driver
about one they had just passed
            painted a pale blue trimmed in white.

It is prison for the insane. (He pronounced it with a hiss:

Priss'n. Then he shook his head, unhappy.) Not prison. It is—

He knotted his face and paused
then cracked open when he found it, smiling and sighing,

                                        Asylum.

o o o

Asylum, he repeated, delighted with the word.

o o o

The passenger looked back through the rear window.
The building seemed to glow in the morning light.
The driver held a compass made of cast-off sounds and letters.

o o o

The passenger is seeking a hut

a possible place of shelter

some remembered form

o o o

of asylum.
                  That evening he takes a ball-
peen hammer smashes the headlights then climbs
in and drives a blind car through blind curves

                          on a road above the sea:

airplanes come in low over the water:

the flickering illumination wipes the road clean.
The car has become a song where he knows the melody

o o o

but not the words.

o o o

It could be a reel about a lamb in a meadow.
It could be a dirge about the loss of a child.

o o o

He takes turns in the back seat
as well as behind the wheel, praying

the song will open its eyes so he
can see the white line in the road

and the green eyes of jackals on the shoulder,
floating like fireflies above roadkill

before dipping back down with moist jaws.

o o o

Inside the asylum
there is a woman

who is luminous
inside her skin.

o o o

The car murmurs along the evening street.
The engine mutters its age with a guttural thrum.

o o o

The woman wears white cotton
underwear and a loose shift.

She sits in the darkness of the courtyard
beneath the greater darkness of a magnolia.

Its waxy leaves are coated with dust
rising from the road beyond the wall.

She hears the sound of the passing motor woven
into the sound of clinking utensils and the chime
of wine glasses being cleared from a table.

Her thoughts are as flat as a table
as she takes a ballpoint pen and copies:

the building sense of momentum

                                   as he entered the strange city

She traces the words
in pale blue ink on white paper.

o o o

Strange might not be the perfect
word for the city
but she has always suspected

there is another one beneath it. Tunneled
with caves and scattered with old bones.

Entering those ruins
to make marks upon the walls
might be the only trick she knows

o o o

and so she lives inside the pale blue

walls. She knows there are no men
with wings, despite the stories.

She does not look to the sky
for gliding silhouettes
to blot out the starlight.

She prefers to become a silence
and filter out through the slatted shutters
into the open

o o o

window of the passing car.

The Sinclair Gift Emporium

The man smiled as the heavy door closed behind him, yet he was perturbed. His palm went flat on the counter, rapping the glass with a gentle clack.

"This doesn't work," he said, then removed his hand to reveal the slender cylinder.

The gesture was somewhat theatrical, as if the shiny silver rod were the fine bone of an android. The clerk looked at the pen and said: "Let's take a look, shall we?" The man nodded his consent, and with a deft twist the clerk removed the cartridge and examined it.

"Perhaps you were unaware this is a custom cartridge?" The clerk raised his eyebrows and waited. When there was no reply, he continued: "You see, this particular ink is silent."

"Silent?" asked the man.

"Yes, silent," said the clerk. "Much like the *t* in listen. Inscrutable, I know, but some of our clients simply can't do without it."

The man stared warily at the clerk who stood behind the counter, his hands folded before him.

"Was this perhaps a gift?" inquired the clerk.

The man nodded, perplexed. "It seems she would have sent a note," he added.

"Perhaps she did," said the clerk with a placid smile.

"You mean—" said the man, his voice trailing off.

"Was there any card at all?" said the clerk. "A blank one, perhaps?"

The man reached into his jacket pocket and withdrew a crisp square of vellum. He studied it, then said: "How exactly does one do it? Do we need a flame to read it, like lemon juice?"

The clerk smiled broadly now, and instantly looked younger. "Not at all. Just cup it over your ear, like this. Then wait. It's more a feeling than anything else."

The man held it lightly, like a delicate leaf, and placed it over his ear. "Good Lord," he said, as his face went strangely still. "She loves me."

Rather Than Read Another Word

Perhaps you could loosen your self within your skin.

After all, you've worn it
since childhood's earliest onset.

No wonder it's grown tight. Soften the muscles around

the eyes and there in your knotted
jaw unclench what's held by habit.

There is no need to talk. Let your tongue grow fat.
Listening can be a balm. Those lines in your head

are still forming, and not of their own accord: we

share the tools that deepen them: emotion, repetition,
emotion, repetition, and the requisite mouthfuls of air.

The Last Expedition

When you settled in the soft silt
of the bottom

you were on your back
looking up through the wavering

water toward the light
and something happened

to your eyes: they grew
solid as the river

stones that line the bank.

Damn, you said,
when we pulled you

dripping from the water,
I can't see. I can't

see at all.
We laid you on the nubbled

deck of the pontoon,
your sodden clothing

wrapping you so tight
your nipples

pushed like fat thorns
through your shirt

and you kept saying
in a calm voice:
I'm blind. I'm completely

blind. We did not
notice the gill-slits

until later
when you began

convulsing on the deck
the thorns grown

into fins
your body one long

muscle as you
flexed and writhed

until you shook
yourself into the green

current and were
gone.

Holder Strand

It was there I discovered him,
the drowned boy

out on the cold flats.
I rolled him over with my boot,

flipping him like a slab.
His dark wet locks

were breaded with sand
and the memory of blue

hovered everywhere
just beneath his skin. It was

me at twelve, I think.
Or maybe thirteen.

The way the sodden
clothing wrapped him

flecked with bits of weed,
the wet jersey pasted

to the wicker of his ribs.
He was raw boned and solemn,

black cuts in his knuckles
from bashing rough rock.

I cannot tell you how long,
how many years have passed

since I have been myself.

Oil and Ash

What's organic emits carbon when burned so animal
dung or dried seaweed picked from rocks or a child left
too long in the sun will all eventually rise toward the place
we used to think God lived: among the clouds on a big chair.

So apparently it's come to this: the way to save the sky is sell
the sky to those who would release ash into it, through pipes.

I understand this economically, and I'd rather not
mention the resemblance to prostitution, but when I open my
mouth it also fills with something called sky, each inhalation
drags sky across the fine hairs of my nostrils stirring them

in patterns resembling the locomotion of centipedes.
The inverted trees of my lungs filter sky into blood a shade

darker than a cardinal, blood so red it seems it should sing.
The seashell whorls of my ears hold barely two-thimbles-
worth of sky but without those twin pockets of stratosphere
thrumming my drums the world would fall as silent as a world

where they had inexplicably fed their own kind into steel machines.
Later, visiting archaeologists might ponder what had driven them

to do such a thing? There might be conjecture about belief systems
or native religions but for the first thousands of years there would be
nothing but the sound of ash sifting through dried leaves, a sound that is
in some ways similar—but also different—from the sound of falling snow.

Look, he said, and pointed

the clouds were different
from the blue ones
that had carried
so much cool rain
and broken the back
of the heat last night

these clouds were
knotted tight
and made of human
limbs and torsos
towering into the sky

that's why
they call it
whether, he said

but no one got it
or if they did
no one cared

because someone
was passing binoculars around

and even though
we all took turns
we could not find
a single entire human

body in that towering cumulus
only different part
after different part

woven tightly
and threatening

to pock the roofs
with bone-hail

and fill the gutters
with warm red rain

Aria

I have a particularly thick shaft
is something a porn star might say
using a deceptively mundane tone
in the midst of a job interview
at a Santa Monica café. He might
slide a Polaroid across the table
nudging aside a basket of hand-cut
fries and a small tin of lemon aioli
so the man in sunglasses could
make sense of his tumescence.

What if that producer began to sing
in gorgeously enunciated Italian
an aria of unornamented intonation
that bespoke genuine emotion
regarding the loneliness of the flesh
caught in a flashbulb and framed
like some sort of battered criminal.

Would the rest of the seated crowd
raise their voice in swollen chorus?
Perhaps the man who slid the picture
would fall to his knees weeping,
astonished at the understanding
finally granted to his member,
astonished to have found himself
crying in a poem about his cock.

from A Natural History of Silence

So many silences: think

the clink of poolside gin and tonics,
ice clattering as it spins in the glass then the underwater

hush of submersion

as you sink below the surface, hair wavering like fire.

o

Also, the sound of bitter words unsaid

hovering in the room like a loosed eel
momentarily stunned in the chill.

o

Then there is the pause of locked eyes
in the midst of lubricious wrangling

o

upstairs, before the shudder.

o

The quiet of the porcelain
cup in the cupboard.

The one with the chipped lip
that never speaks.

The blue-green stillness
of the robin's egg

discarded from the nest.

The silence
of the loaded gun.

o

The silence of stone
differing, quietly, from the silence of iron.

o

The cello groaning
into the tuned calm

that precedes the song.

o

Beneath the pines
a single needle falls. It

ticks into the duff.

o

What about the slender
nothing between the next

two words.

o

Or the endless inhalation
before the piercing air-horn

o

scream of the wounded child?

o

Then there is the silence
of truth unspoken. The muteness

of rust on barbed wire. Or the general quiet

of you

reading this: the silence of the birdbath
waiting for rain.

Unspoken

Given the unspeakable nature of their differences,
they decided to settle their divorce in mime court.

It was a pale imitation of justice, but all in all
we agreed the testimony rang true. Outside,

the shadows of the houses swallowed
the shadows of the pigeons without flinching.

Some things are easier to absorb than others,
said the judge, using white gloves and what

we finally understood to be an invisible rope.
Before that he'd been trapped in a glass box

which most likely represented the transparent
vows they'd first spoken on that rainy June day,

back when we were so concerned with our finery
we missed the nerves wired under the words.

From Chaos

I.

Listen and tinsel wrestled,
and silent inlets were born.

Still water opened before us,
there, off the coast of Bologna.
The hourglass held falling snow
and gentle was the root of genital.

This Latin mispronunciation
stemmed from the ancient decree:
Tenderly touch what is tender,
and often you will feel better.

A fork of geese dragged the sky
with hoarse and rasping wings.
The sound was a lone thing
in the blank and open air.

II.

And suddenly it seemed you wanted to be a part from my collection
and apart from me. I could not tell if you meant this
in an underhanded way, and thus became utterly whelmed.

Calm down, you said. Render seizures unto Caesar.

If only such things were aloud, said the mime offhandedly.
He'd wandered in searching for conclusions,
and his gesture was little more than a white-gloved shiver.

How lovely, you motioned back, with a nearly silent
murmur. Listen. It ends as it begins.

What Might

It all begins with *might*, the word
and its power, which might make
right unless it's the muscular sort
and then we're talking otherwise.

We might begin again, I think,
without losing one another,
given these current arrangements,
given that we're talking

about possibilities, about mights,
about one poem with two beginnings
and the many dozen doorways
that we don't walk through each day

opening up a permanent and shadowy
elsewhere, a space where one man
can spend his entire life beside himself,
inhabiting two houses on the same street,

happily eating an orange in one room,
weeping softly to himself in another,
breathing soundly in both places at once,
and of course it is the weeping man

who might be happy, pushed toward it
by Casals coaxing something eternal
from the emptiness of his cello,
while the man eating the orange might

be ticking toward some sort of pain,
carefully separating peel from fruit,

one sweet section after another,
oblivious to what could be happening

to a wife and daughter elsewhere:
a small indignity perhaps, a rudeness,
or maybe something darker. But as it is,
his pleasure multiplies with each

bursting bite, *Oranges are miracles*,
he thinks, envisioning himself
a contented monk in a sunlit cell
which in the way of cells soon divides

again and again, until he's imagined
an entire monastery of robed brethren
chanting vespers and stooping in the fields
each one of them wearing a rough garment

and wondering how it came to be
that he found himself so far from home
filling his basket with tender lavender
in the mind of a man he's never met.

September Picnic

Ever get the feeling you've been cheated?
—JOHN LYDON

It was a September picnic
and in the splintered basket
purchased cheap
as trucks and tents were being loaded and packed
the fruit spotty, ready for wasps
but wonderfully fragrant
were pears.

Pears from the open-air market
overripe in a damp brown bag.

The fragile leather of their skin
spiraled from the horn-handled
knife in grandfather's hands
knotted and working
with the thoughtless
efficiency of six decades
twirling out damp garlands
to drape our fingers.

We were on the train, crossing the St. Lawrence,
heading into the sunburnt fields beyond Montreal.
We were eating pears. Slices lifted wetly from the blade.

The train clacking and the picnic not yet begun and this
is nonetheless all that I can recall. I remember only the pears.
We could draw conclusions about anticipation, or about joy.

Or that possibly only sweetness persists
but this would trouble me all the more because
this memory is not mine. It belongs to Moses Herzog

who in turn owes it to Saul Bellow who wrote him
into life and placed him in a book that I read and never forgot
and now, yes, I remember the pears. I can taste them,

even, after all these years that never passed
between me and that honeyed moment.

Interrogation

What utensil would you use to eat a bowl of rain?
How many policemen does it take to make a candle?
Where is the pelvic bone of a centaur located?
How many policemen does it take in general? Nine?
Doesn't that strike you as more than enough? What if
one of them is named Wick and the other Tallow?
Could their marriage be called a candle? Does that
complicate the uniform? If one were the front
of the centaur would the hind end dream of goats?
When I mentioned a bowl of rain earlier was it clear

that I meant a bowl constructed solely out of raindrops
and not a conventional bowl holding collected rainwater?
Now when I mention a bowl of rain is it perfectly clear?
Clear as the fallen rain? Rain settled in a puddle that holds
pale drowned earthworms because for one fatal moment
they mistook that clear panel of water for a long deep drink
and did not recognize it as the vessel of their demise?
Why does drink hold the demise of so many? Are we
there yet? Will we ever be there? How can we truly know?
What would the earthworm tell us with its pale tiny mouth?

Lions

If a lion could speak, we could not understand him.
— WITTGENSTEIN

the problem would not be those beautiful
teeth or the dark purse
of his mouth muffling consonants
or the complete absence of adjectives
but rather how his tense
always slides through time
loose as a brushstroke
shading every action into now

and there would be the arrival of one word
for blood riding the wind
and another for the shuddering
twitch of the hindquarters that presages the burst
before sudden fangs make meat go slack

also that volatile purr
coughing and guttering
like candle flame in the breeze

as well as the unnerving jokes ending in splinters
of marrow and cracked bone
and the confusion of sixty-two

different words for hunger
each one opening
into the same fearful roar

but only the one
telling silence
for sleep

A Woman Stands in a Field

The scene is so clear it might be a memory.

But no. It is too clear for that. This is something happening right now.

A woman stands in a field near the only stand of trees for a long way round. She is looking down, scanning the ground. Perhaps she is searching for acorns.

But she is beyond the tree-shadow, and she has no basket in which to gather, and besides, upon closer inspection, it turns out the trees are not even oaks. She parts the grass with her hands, gently, as a mother might push the hair from her child's forehead. She steps gingerly over the rooms and tunnels filled with tiny animals. A wind comes. It shakes the tree and runs its hand across the field, flattening the grass.

This evening, she will still be here. It will be hard to see the lesser darkness of her dress bobbing above the greater darkness of the field.

Days from now, when she finds it, we will no longer be watching. She will draw it gently from the thatch, glinting like a baby snake, a thin gold chain.

There you are, she will say matter-of-factly. She will examine the clasp carefully and then refasten the chain around her neck and begin walking through the fields toward home. It is just as well that we will no longer be observing the scene. Her faith in the clasp seems almost perverse, and it would be all you could do not to cry out.

The Crisis

The financier walked into a roomful of women, scantily clad in lacy underthings. They were all quite heavyset, and their amplitude appealed to him. He became aroused.

"What is it that you want from us?" they murmured, as he walked among them. "It seems we were summoned here specifically for you."

"How do you know this to be the case?" he asked, gently brushing the hair from one woman's shoulder.

"Because none of us remember anything other than this room."

He paused and looked around him. Many of the women appeared to be just coming awake, blinking lazily on their velvet couches. One smiled at him and arched her back, stretching. "So you remember nothing at all?"

"Nothing. It's as if we were born five minutes ago. Or five hours. There are no clocks here. All we know is this room, and waiting."

"For me," he said.

There was no reply. The women exchanged glances. There was not one among them that could tell him they had no navels, no scars. Their bodies were like those of dolls, a smooth pink flatness rounding down the belly and around, unbroken.

Elpenor

There was a man, Elpenor, the youngest in our ranks,
none too brave in battle, none too sound in mind.
      —BOOK 10, *THE ODYSSEY*

There he is, standing on the granite shingle, watching
a sail recede across the bright water, no larger than a swan.

The shouts that laced his dreams were preparations for departure.
He nuzzled into sleep, forgotten. Useless to raise his voice now,
yet the cries of the gulls cut sharply. He feels the morning breeze
blow through him like a ladder. He does not yet know that he is

dead, having run so hurriedly out of his broken-necked body.
But when he wanders back and sees the spine angled like a
snapped twig, the earth around soaked dark, he turns and runs
toward the glinting water and across the heaving waves, leaving

no tracks on their rolling hills, crying, *Wait! I'm here. I'm still here!*

Look, Overlook

The wing
of a moth: fine ridges, dusty translucence, powdery
crumbling as it feathers between two
fingers: you

are made of such soft stuff, crumbling
beneath breath;
the dust on your things, your bookshelves and shoes, was once

skin, and your day of long walking is
done, not done

through wet grass, shadows, and

sight: the starling-spangled elm, the hinges of your hand, clouds

sledding on the wind.

The Dark Thing

It used to come into the light,
so deeply creased it seemed to be scarred,
bristling with hairs like a baby elephant.

Its hunger was slow and stolid but also
always there, tusks clicking above its steady
jaws as it moved among the trees.

Seeing the limit of its skin lessened it—
the way it lightened into pinkness near the lips
unnerved us. We hurled rocks and broken

concrete, even poked it with sticks
we'd blackened in the fire. When the first blade
cut and drew a startling thread of blood,

it moaned so quietly we backed away.
It sounds like my grandmother in her sleep,
someone whispered. We looked

at one another. The thing was barely
moving. Then the boy who'd spoken
unstrapped the knife from the stick, wiped it

clean on the grass and folded it
shut with a sharp click. That's enough,
he said. It had been so much

easier than we'd imagined.
This is what we would have said,
if we had spoken of it again.

The Book of _____

First, there is the consideration of my appearance which even those
who care for me say is troublesome. It is not simply the coarseness
of hair coming from where one does not anticipate hair, but also
things beneath the surface that stretch the skin and hinges that work
differently, so I am both more and less mobile than your kind and though
I've learned to walk upright as a man, when I'm alone I scuttle sideways.

I am quite fast. I hope I can say this without boasting. I am told
I appear more liquid than solid when I wend across a room, feathering
over couches, tables and other obstructions rather than walking round.
Uneven surfaces disturb me no more than trees disturb the wind.
People do not tell me these things in admiration but as explanation
for the fear that glitters in their eyes. I try to speak softly but my voice

breaks like glass. When they found me, I was feeding on venison. A doe,
toppled on the roadside and risen in the afternoon sun. I kept my vigil
until dusk, then scissored slowly up the bank and started in. I was young.
Headlights astonished me. I was docile, easily taken. The whole escapade
leaves me with a feeling of vague shame and chagrin, especially now
that I've learned to read and can place the incident on the shelf of context.

I have a window in my room overlooking the garden from which I see
the crowns of trees, and in the evening the sunset gilds the rooftops then
stretches a blanket of shadow across them until darkness eats the world.
They were kind enough to tint the window for me so that I can see
out but no one can see in which might sound like a lonely thing to say
but I understand. I have foresworn using my pincers to sever the cordage

of my meals though knife and fork feel dull as cold toes. Yet the fear
remains in others' eyes and is there always, so much so that I wonder
if it is not unfounded. I have dreams. Some I am not inclined to share,
but there is one that continues to return and seems innocent enough.

It seems to spring from your world more than mine and I wonder if you might be willing to interpret its signs. I cannot tell it with words but must

write the dream upon the world with my body. I have been waiting to do this for a long time. My joints ache to unfurl. You were kind to listen. Let me offer my dream in return. Open the door. Let me out.

Nuns

Have you heard the one about the nun and the penguin
in the bathtub and the nun drops the soap
and says to the penguin, Do you think you could
fish that out? And the penguin says, What do you think I am,

a radio? We used to tell it in school, everyone
standing in a circle and laughing like jackals, except for the one
not in on the joke, which in this particular poem
is you, because it's not a joke at all

just a misleading non sequitur
designed to bait the unwitting

into falling into laughter alongside everyone else
so they could then be turned upon and savagely asked:

What's so fucking funny?

As we watched them squirm to explain, grasping
at the tuxedoed symmetry of nuns and penguins,
the real laughter thundered out and made it
clear how much we'd learned.

The Shop Across the Street

I walked outside and looked to where the sky used to be.
The new laminate is better than I feared, I murmured,
but why this watery yellow? Why not sky blue?

The president's voice crackled over the loudspeakers
and announced that yellow was *something-something*
but the spatter of white noise drowned him out.

The shop across the street—the one that sells clay figurines—
was not much help. Did you understand the president?
I asked, a little out of breath from running across the avenue.

The storekeeper smiled and said,
I am not able to recognize the president
even when I look right at him.

How much is that, I said, pointing at a figurine,
a little man, posed on a shelf behind him.

Oh, that one is not for sale.
                              Why not?
Because it's me.

I leaned across the counter to peer at the tiny face
and saw that it was true: a perfect likeness. Well, I said,
whirling to leave, I guess now we know who the whore is.

The People Who Came Afterward

lived oblivious to the drifting veils of rain.
There were no fences. The point of existence
was to gather things in concentric rings
so possessions formed the hive where you lived.
It was the most effective prison ever devised
by humans. When the downpour came to melt
it away, filling depressions with grit and soft clay,
pottery shards returned to their element—bones
came unbound. Glass rose like fins from the ground.

The Professional

She arrived in a dark suit and a mask-like smile, explaining
her services in a manner so polished it almost put us off.
This is my specialty, she soothed. Both mind and house
will be empty as a mountain wind once I'm done. I sensed
she'd said those words before. We sat at the kitchen table,
you and I, looking at one another, hoping the other felt more
certain, more assured. Once we signed, it would take years
before we acknowledged our mistake. She'd left the whole day
open, and could begin immediately. Was there perhaps a guest
room where she could change? Her assistant arrived with
a black duffel, fresh white towels, and a stainless-steel basin.

I didn't know the basin would be so big, I murmured.
We looked at one another warily. It isn't always a clean process,
she reassured. You do understand, once I'm sequestered, it is
very important that I not be disturbed. We nodded. She closed
the door with an audible click. For the first few hours, it seemed
okay. Her assistant sat out in the van, with the windows down,
reading. We sat in the living room and tried to do the same,
ignoring the sounds coming from the guest room, sighs that
sharpened into cries. When a few faces started disappearing
in the photographs above the piano, you leapt to your feet.
This isn't right, you said. These things shouldn't be removed.

But what about the pain? I asked. Don't you want it gone?
No, you said, pointing to the image of a child, suddenly frantic.
The eyes had faded to nothing. From forehead to cheekbone
was just smooth skin. I ran to the window. The van was gone,
as was the tire swing that had been there an hour earlier. I looked
and saw the elm losing its limbs, one by one. Maybe we can still
get some of our money back, I said. And then you said: I want her
gone. The assistant had sealed the door shut with tape. It came

off with a spattering sound, and the shrieks from inside paused. Then the voice came, a strangled croak as I opened the door and saw her, smaller than I remembered, perched on the dresser, her suit pooled on the floor beneath her. Her face had become a sort of beak, hinged open and hissing. But it was the children that were upsetting, sitting in a circle at her feet, quietly singing.

Imperfection

after Tomaž Šalamun

Leather without history
is merely the skin of the dead

animals that once walked these fields.
Strength without rickets

can be seen on any playground.
Consider the appetite

of these children and remember:
blood is silk.

Walk silently away. Drop your empty
cup in the receptacle. Note

how the plastic helmet is stained brown
from where your lips drew coffee

out with a wet sound. *Blood is like fruit.*
Maybe spend a moment

thinking about the tanks and hunger
but keep moving.

There is no need to thrash yourself.
I know a doctor who can pull that

wire clean from your back. We
will roar and get excited soon enough.

The Horse

When it says The Horse up there in letters slightly larger than
these including that beautifully balanced H that could serve as
a solid frame for a barn door and that s curving from the back
of the e in rather uncanny imitation of how a horsetail curves up
from meaty rump before falling downward in a swoop, you might
think of a glossy coat rippling over musculature bred to quickness
rather than the stiff and bloated thing toppled sideways in the ditch

that we saw as we rolled downhill into the warm and humid sea air
letting dusty mountains recede behind us with all that endless agave
that tinged field after field with something much softer than blue.

A family in a small red wagon: the girl eight, the boy almost five,
the beach below us home for a week after nearly nine hours driving
getting slightly lost in Guadalajara and suddenly two legs jutting like
poles across the road and a man with a blue T-shirt wrapped across his
face and sawing through the bone with the rusted buck blade kicking
out a little pink powder with every pull and the smell mingling with
green air and ripened mangos as we swerved momentarily into the
oncoming lane and I looked at the barrel of those ribs swollen tight
wondering about the gush of gas and stink if it were pierced when

the boy asked in a tremulous voice if that was a horse and before
anyone could think what to say the girl answered, Not anymore.

Now Here, Nowhere

The cow unfolds its legs and
rises against the white sky,
flickering among the tree trunks

as we pass. The window
glass is cold against my forehead
and I can feel the pavement

humming below.
A pine has overturned, roots
ripped into the air. A dog

trots along the road, another
lies dead on the shoulder, fur
frozen to the pavement like carpet.

We drive on, not telling
how a dusting of snow
whitens shadows, it is still cold but

water will run, insects will rise,
these dogs will flower
in sweet decay. We pass

another broken tree,
the heartwood split
open in a storm.

The car swings
through rolling curves
beneath the white sky,

the sky that holds clouds and light
and clouds and light and nowhere
does it explain.

In the Pasture Corner

The earth beneath the oak is boar-broken,
torn dark and furrowed, clods unearthed
in a dirt-spray: fine roots stand up like hairs.
There, where hooves churned turf to mud
the gash is greased red with blood: the flung
lamb snagged heavy on the branch a hair
too high for the muscle of what pounded
the earth and pounded the earth beneath it.

How It Survived for a While

It waited until we wandered home, then
limped to the sea where the rasping
mouths of hagfish cleaned its wounds.

For a while it disguised itself
as a hailstorm, but the constant
clattering loosened its teeth and the cold

became too difficult to bear.
It chose instead to become a forest thing,
gifted at disappearing. Yet it was

the trees themselves that gave it away,
frightened that one of them
had somehow learned to walk.

Now it will become our king! they whispered,
wrapping their roots like rope
tighter and tighter around its thick neck.

The School

The anaconda was useful. The youngest
obeyed more readily and occasionally
did not return from the boiler room.

The older children paid attention
to lessons in toolmaking and chemistry,
forming acids that scald, then used boar-
bristle brushes to outline the boundaries of their lives.

Wolverines were introduced, worrying
carrion out on the playing fields. Then
jackals. We watched them seize viscera
and tug, quivering the whole of the rubbery
carcass, shredding the body into ragged skeins
as the steady rain fell. When the teacher intoned

Nature red in tooth and claw, we understood.
They were out there, weaving drunkenly
among the puddles, fur flecked with mud, our parents
waiting in the road beyond: a line of black cars, idling.

The Orangutan

They were more than a little embarrassed when it turned out their orangutan was electric.

They've gotten so good with the musculature, said father, who knew?

Also the soft parts, said mother, who loved to stroke the wrinkled skin in the hinges of his body. Sometimes his flesh responded in the most surprising ways. And lord knows, she added, he ate more than his share of bananas.

But then they found them, mashed in a brown pile, a syrupy mass stashed behind the furnace in the basement. He had always been a furtive monkey. Dozens of ants were trapped in the clear fluid leaking from the pile.

We couldn't have come up with a better trap if we'd tried, shouted father, picking at the delicate carcasses.

Their daughter remained quiet through it all, which they attributed to shock. When the baby was born some months later, its face was eerily reminiscent of a calculator.

I don't know what to say, the girl announced, pressing the function key on her new son. Every time I run the numbers, I get a different answer.

Manhood

Sherman tried to show the extent of his manhood
by insisting his wife wear the pants in the family.
This allowed his manhood to extend
well below his knees, wrinkled as the head of a vulture,
and then coil damply beneath him
as he settled onto the porch steps to read the paper.

I'd be more inclined to apologize for that image
were it not for the fact that the buzzard head
was at one time attached to the body of a snake
replete with a simile evoking crinkled hosiery
and thus this is the mild version and contains
significantly fewer genital-animal parallels
which editors do not typically recommend
for inclusion in general-interest publications.

Why there was only one sturdy pair of pants
between the two of them remains a mystery.

And that those pants were stitched of leather
with supple creases worked into their knees
and embroidered detailing on the pockets
is perhaps as close as we will get to the reason
for their existence in the first place. At this point
it would probably be wiser to return to Sherman
reading on the porch, nude from the waist down.

Yet nude would be an overstatement
given the pair of tire-tread sandals he is wearing
which of course have the effect of making him
even nuder—which is not a word—but was

nonetheless included for purposes of double entendre,
just as the sandals were conjured to amplify his nudity.

And look, there is his unnamed wife doing some
gritty task, mussing the knees of those disturbing pants
as she vigorously trowels the root-base of her rosebush.
I'm sweating like a pig in these trousers, she mutters,
not to him exactly, though there is no one else there.

He is so long in responding it seems the moment
might pass when the newspaper rustles and he says,
Fine . . . give them here . . . I'll wear the damn things,
sighing like a beleaguered king who must wear pants
he does not like, rank with the sweat of his wife,
shoveling his soft flesh into that leather that pinches
like church shoes on a child's feet in August.

Foretold

he shot the bird through the eye
then plucked the pouch

of the belly clean and cut it

open with scissors
so the gut breathed

steam in the chill air

Could you read these for me? he asked
pulling gray-pink strings from inside

Boy or girl? and will the labor be easy?

It seems an odd way
of finding such a thing out, I said

but I think you can wager
on a cesarean

and the child will not go
hungry

Binary

He wore a slightly rumpled shirt,
its buttoned placket off by one
so a triangle of cloth flapped loose
over his belt buckle. It struck me
this was possibly a studied move
meant to indicate joie de vivre.
He set his coffee down with a clack,
sat in the chair opposite and said,
"How would you like to be a zero

in a world of ones," and he paused
like that after the zero, for effect
yet did not wait to see what effect
this tidbit of drama would generate
before plunging forward in what was
either intellectual vigor or arrogance:

"As a zero in the Arabic numeral system
you could increase by tenfold the value
of any *one* you chose to stand beside.
And as a zero in a binary world of ones
you would quite literally contain
within the orb of your nothingness
half of all the instrumental information
needed to reduce the world's chaos
into straightforward propositions."

He smiled broadly and settled back
in his chair to await the response,
and that is when I slowly raised

my revolver level with his chest
to help him understand the world
is not in love with certainty.

Recollection

Sometimes, after waking,
I take a moment to collect myself.

My mind wanders to the cabinet
where I keep one leg neatly folded,

held snug by a canvas strap.

The other is toppled like
firewood beside the bed.

The embroidered box on the bedside table
that once housed a blown-glass ornament

now holds my tongue,
that dark knot of sleeping muscle.

My pale twinned arms
lie nestled together in a battered cello case

fingers tangled like amorous starfish.

The cradle of my pelvis sits on a wooden saddle
designed specifically for that purpose

and the hairy coil of my privates
rests on the dresser, next to a pile of coins.

How I'm writing this is anyone's guess.

I've always been somewhat
scattered in dismembered places,

maybe you can remember
                            and mis-
take me, yes,
              take me for my assemblage.

The Last Time I Saw God

was different from the first two times.

I'd fallen asleep and when I woke
it was just the two of us rocking
gently through each rumbling curve.

(It was on a subway car at night.)

I thought you'd be a woman, I said.

You always say that, he said and laughed.

Because I always think it, I said.
Every time I see you is the first time.

He shrugged: *That's just how it works.*

That is when I noticed his slight
resemblance to my father,

which also always happens.
Aren't we ever going to stop?

I asked, suddenly aware
of the hurtling train.

He just looked at me.
That was when I knew.

Acknowledgments

32 Poems: "What Might"
10 x 3: "The Difficulty of Holding Time"
Beechers: "Imperfection"
Beloit Poetry Journal: "The Field Beyond the Wall"
Blackbird: "Aria," "Manhood," "The School"
The Chattahoochee Review: "Look, Overlook"
Denver Syntax: "Rather Than Read Another Word"
Forklift, Ohio: "Memory"
Green Mountains Review: "Binary," "The Last Time I Saw God," "from
A Natural History of Silence," "Unspoken"
Guernica: "Oil and Ash"
Literary Imagination: "Elpenor"
The Literary Review: "Lions"
The Los Angeles Review: "The Book of _____"
New Ohio Review: "The Professional"
Oxford Poetry: "Soirée"
The Paris-American: "A Woman Stands in a Field"
Phoebe: "The Dark Thing," "How It Survived for a While"
Prairie Schooner: "In the Pasture Corner," "The People Who Came
Afterward"
Rattle: "The Last Expedition"
Redivider: "The Orangutan"
Salamander: "After Machado"
Smartish Pace: "September Picnic"
Swarm: "The Horse"
Weber: "Now Here, Nowhere"
Whiskey Island: "Clockwatcher," "Interrogation"

"Oil and Ash" and "September Picnic" previously appeared in the
chapbook *The Imaginary City* (OW! Arts 2012).

MICHAEL BAZZETT's poems have appeared in *Ploughshares, Massachusetts Review, Pleiades, 32 Poems, Hayden's Ferry Review,* and *Best New Poets.* He is the author of the chapbook *The Imaginary City* (OW! Arts 2012), and the winner of the Bechtel Prize from Teachers & Writers Collaborative. A longtime member of the faculty at The Blake School, Bazzett lives in Minneapolis with his wife and two children.

MILKWEED EDITIONS

and

THE LINDQUIST & VENNUM
FOUNDATION

are pleased to announce the third award of

THE LINDQUIST & VENNUM
PRIZE FOR POETRY

to

MICHAEL BAZZETT

Established in 2011, the annual Lindquist & Vennum Prize for
Poetry awards $10,000 and publication by Milkweed Editions
to a poet residing in North Dakota, South Dakota, Minnesota,
Iowa, or Wisconsin. Finalists are selected from among all
entrants by the editors of Milkweed Editions. The winning
collection is selected annually by an independent judge.
The 2014 Lindquist & Vennum Prize for Poetry was judged
by Kevin Prufer.

Milkweed Editions is one of the nation's leading independent
publishers, with a mission to identify, nurture and publish
transformative literature, and build an engaged community
around it. The Lindquist & Vennum Foundation was
established by the Minneapolis-headquartered law firm of
Lindquist & Vennum, PLLP, and is a donor-advised fund of
The Minneapolis Foundation.

Design & typesetting by Mary Austin Speaker

Typeset in Bembo

Bembo is a revival typeface created in 1929 for Monotype based upon the humanist design cut by Francesco Griffo in the late fifteenth century. The design first appeared in print in 1496 with the publication of *Petri Bembi de Aetna Angelum Chabrielem liber*, a text by Italian humanist poet Pietro Bembo.